THE WALK OF A SINNER; YET SAVED

The Walk of A Sinner; Yet Saved

PROPHETESS NAKISHA RUPERT

Superior Publishing LLC.

Contents

Dedication	vi
Acknowledgments	1
INTRODUCTION	2
1. LOOKING BACK	4
2. A DOWNWARD SPIRAL	11
3. LUPUS: A DEATH SENTENCE	18
4. ENVY, JEALOUSY, WITHCRAFT & A Baby	25
5. NEW HOUSE, NEW CAR, ACCEPTING MY CALLING & ADULTERY	37
CONCLUSION	46

This book is dedicated to Carolyn Orr. Thanks woman of God for always being there for me and my family. Your words of wisdom and Godly council over the years has shaped me into the woman of God I am. I prayed that God would send me someone that could help me to grow in him and he sent me you. I thank God for you.

Copyright © 2022 by Prophetess Nakisha Rupert
Copyright © 2022 pictures by Jar'Quez Bradshaw

ISBN/SKU 978-1-953056-28-3
EISBN 978-1-953056-29-0

All rights reserved. No part of this book may be reproduced in any manner whatsoever without written permission except in the case of brief quotations embodied in critical articles and reviews.

SUPERIOR PUBLISHING, 2022
CEDAR BLUFF, MS
(662) 295-9893

Acknowledgments

To my husband:
I love the man God has made you, continue to look to God for EVERYTHING!!!

To my sons:
Ja'Marcus, Jar'Quez, Ja'Kerrick trust God in ALL that you do.
I love all of you and thank God for you.

INTRODUCTION

As I look back over my life, God has really been grooming me for the Woman of God I am now, and he is still not finished. It took me getting to where I am now to fully understand why everything that I went through was not about me and how I felt about the situation but who God was molding me to be. See, if God had not allowed me to go through different trials and heartbreaks, I would not be able to have the anointing that God has given me. I would not be able to tell someone going through certain situations how to get through them. Yes, I know I could tell them God did it but like my war sister Carolyn say, "Don't tell me God will make a way and leave it at that but tell me what you had to do for God to get you through it!" Meaning, tell me what scripture to read, what prayer to pray, when to praise Him, when to stand still and when to put on the full armor of the Lord.

I have learned over the 40 years of my life that the things I went through were not because of something I did, but because of someone I was going to have to help in the kingdom of God. I remember so many times asking God why me? Lord what did I do to deserve so much pain because it was painful? Only to hear God tell me it is not about you, but about the people I am sending to you. He had to explain to me that I could not help anyone if I had not been through it myself. He said, "How are you going to be able to tell them how to get through if you have not been through it yourself?" He told me He could not use me the way He needed to if I had not experienced the hurt and the pain. I had to go through the storm in order to tell someone going through the storm how to get out of it. I could not go off hearsay, I had to experience the hurt and the pain to get the anointing.

    In this book I will be opened to letting you experience the pain that I went through. How many days I was in sackcloth and ashes, broken but God mended me back together again. If it were not for His grace and mercy I would not be here. The Devil tried to kill me several times but GOD!! Over the next few chapters I will share with you some of the most heart wrenching times of my life. It was painful but worth it because I now know WHO I AM AND MOST IMPORTANTLY WHOSE I AM. When you know WHOSE you are and that EVERYTHING is POSSIBLE with Him, then and only then is when you know you can make it.

Chapter 1

LOOKING BACK

When I have my alone time with the Father, sometimes in my prayer room or just riding in my car, He always shows me how He has always had His hand on my life. The earliest I can remember is, when my sister died. I was only 10 years old when I lost my best friend. Being so young, I didn't understand death. I remember feeling so numb and asking my grandmother why she had to die. My grandmother told me that God had a garden and in this garden, there were many flowers that represented us. She said that when God was ready for us to come to live with Him, He would pick our flower because we were special. It was a pain that I just could not understand at the time. I can barely understand now at times because I loved her so much.

Even at a young age, I remember God talking to me. At first, I did not know who the voice was but as time went by my grandmother told me it was God. I remember before she died, we were in the hospital after the car accident waiting to hear from the doctors. My mother and aunt had come to Alabama after hearing about the wreck. My sister was in critical condition, but my mom thought it was me. I still remember turning around seeing her and my aunt's face when they saw me standing in the hall of the hospital. They were relieved to see me standing with just an arm brace on but on the inside, I was afraid, scared and numb. I had not seen my sister since the scene of the wreck. My mom said that we were going to a room to stay the night until morning then we would find out about her condition. I remember telling my mama I was scared and her telling me that we were going to pray and that my sister would be alright. This was the first time I really prayed. I did the whole getting on my knees and begging God to let my sister be alright. That morning when we got the news, I was devastated. No one explained to me that it had to be in God's will for my sister to live. This was my first real pain, my real loss of someone I never thought I would lose.

I remember traveling back to my Big Ma's house. My cousins and I were outside where my Big Ma had an old iron like horse and carriage in her yard, and I was there crying and asking God why? Family members were telling me you are not supposed to ask God why. Now that I am older, and have read the Bible for myself, the words of Jesus in Mark, "when you do not understand why something happen it's ok to ask God for wisdom knowledge and understanding to what is going on."

But back to the day she died, I was hurting, and I feel God allowed me to see my sister standing by that carriage in a white dress with a bright light shining on her. After seeing her, a great sense of calming peace came over me. Even though I was still sad, I knew she was in heaven with

God and He had truly picked her flower from His garden to be with Him. After God allowed me to see that, I went on to having dreams and visions about things and they would come to pass.

I remember dreaming that both my grandma and Big Ma were in each other's body, but both were telling me that they were going to die and how they would die. One by heart attack and one by being struck by lightning. I have always heard that when you dream about a person its always someone else. Well, a month after dreaming this my grandfather died of a heart attack, two months later my aunt was struck by lightning on Labor Day.

Not even a year later, I was going to summer school to take my English so that I could leave school early my twelfth-grade year, I had a dream that I had stolen my mama's car. And I drove it to pick up my friends to skip summer school to go to Columbus. On our way to Columbus, I hit the Tombigbee bridge. And in this dream, I could see myself floating to the bottom of the river. That same day, I went to school and my friends were like, "Where is the car?" I told them about the dream only to be picked up from school by my aunt and her husband to find out my other aunt had hit a bridge and drowned. Those were just a few of the dreams and visions I felt God was showing me to prepare me for the day He would really show me things. At this point in my life, I was a teenager, 15 or 16 years old and having to experience so much. But I learned, it was not to break me, but it was to make me.

By the time I was 19, I was married and had one son, Ja'Marcus. Then we had two more sons Jar'Quez and Ja'Kerrick. This marriage did not last long. There was a lot of infidelity and fighting. I could not continue to be in a marriage where my sons were always seeing me and their father fighting. It was 2003, when my son Ja'Kerrick was born. Later that year, I would lose what felt like my soul, my grandma, the woman I called mama. This was a pain I could not deal with. I felt defeated. I felt like this was the last straw! She was one of the women that taught me everything. How to be a woman, how to cook, clean, mother, but most of all about God. She used to always tell me that God always made a way. She said she never went without of anything because of Him. I watched her over the years bury her husband then two of her daughters, raise all 6 of their kids while fighting cancer to losing everything in a house fire. She never complained, she held on to her faith and kept trusting God. Even though I never saw her ask why or complain, she used to say that if God allowed it to happen then He would bring her through. I remember looking at her some days wondering how she was still able to smile after so much loss. I did not understand then, but I do now. Her dying sent me down a downward spiral. I begin to smoke weed like never before, popping pills a lot of things that I am not proud of. I know God allowed me to go through those things now for a reason. But, He never took His hand off me.

When I look back at some nights, I would start drinking on Friday and would not stop until Monday morning. I would be rolling out of my mind. There were nights me and my friends would be so high we would ride until the sun came up. There were times when on a Saturday night we would party so hard that we would party right in to church the next morning still high from the night before. When I say I know I should be dead and gone, I mean just that. BUT

GOD!! He had a plan that I knew not of, the Devil was trying to kill me. The Devil had already peaked into my future and seen what God had in stored for me. His plans were to KILL, STEAL AND DESTROY ME and everything around me. BUT GOD!

During this time, I was dating my now husband, Quincy. I remember the day before my grandma died, me begging her not to leave me. I remember her telling me I was going to be alright and me telling her to just wait on me the next morning I would pick her up and bring her back to the doctor to get her blood transfusion because her blood was low. I remember her saying you going to be alright you are going to have somebody to be there for you. I believe to this day she was talking about Quincy. My grandma died November 21, 2003 and, on this day, Quincy being my best guy friend at the time told me he was in love with me.

Now

here is where the story jumps.... See you in chapter two!!!!

The Word of God that helped me through this time:
THE HOLY BIBLE
MATTHEW 11:28- 30;
28 "Come to me, all you who are weary and burdened, and I will give you rest. 29 Take my yoke upon you and learn from me, for I am gentle and humble in heart, and you will find rest for your souls. 30 For my yoke is easy and my burden is light."

PSALM 147:33
He heals the brokenhearted and binds up their wounds.

1 THESSALONIANS 4:13-18;
13 Brothers and sisters, we do not want you to be uninformed about those who sleep in death, so that you do not grieve like the rest of mankind, who have no hope. 14 For we believe that Jesus died and rose again, and so we believe that God will bring with Jesus those who have fallen asleep in him. 15 According to the Lord's word, we tell you that we who are still alive, who are left until the coming of the Lord, will certainly not precede those who have fallen asleep. 16 For the Lord himself will come down from heaven, with a loud command, with the voice of the archangel and with the trumpet call of God, and the dead in Christ will rise first. 17 After that, we who are still alive and are left will be caught up together with them in the clouds to meet the Lord in the air. And so, we will be with the Lord forever. 18 Therefore encourage one another with these words.

JOSHUA 1:9 -
9 Have I not commanded you? Be strong and courageous. Do not be afraid; do not be discouraged, for the LORD your God will be with you wherever you go."

ROMANS 8:28 -
28 And we know that in all things God works for the good of those who love him, who have been called according to his purpose.

MATTHEW 5:4 -
4 Blessed are those who mourn, for they will be comforted.

Chapter 2

A DOWNWARD SPIRAL

This is where the drugs became an everyday thing. My drug of choice was weed, ecstasy pills, and drinking. It was crazy because even though I would be high I was conscious about what I was doing and the decisions I was making. I was basically trying to numb the pain of losing my grandma.

THEN life really got bad! My aunt, who was raised like my sister, by mama died. I did not see it coming because I felt like I was so distant from God with all the drugs and stuff. In my mind, I was still going to church and praying occasionally, but I could no longer hear God. I was not reading His word. I was just living blindly. I had lost everyone who I deemed loved me, flaws and all. At this point, I was two years into helping the Devil kill me.

Two more years had passed before I started NOT wanting to smoke or pop pills. I can say that was one thing I was glad about, that I was never addicted to drugs but it was a choice thing. I took them because I wanted too, not because I needed them. Not even realizing, that in the midst of my foolishness, God was protecting me even then. I say that because I did not get to a point of needing it to where I stole to get it. I sit sometimes and think about how people would get laced and go crazy. I never smoked with anyone I did not know. I always rolled my own blunt. But still so much could have went wrong. Every weekend I was in somebody's club, and then it got to where I did not need a club I would party at home.

I got to a point to where I started feeling empty. I knew what I was missing. But at this time, I felt like I could not get back to God. The devil had me feeling like I had done too much. I had gotten mad too much at God and He would not forgive me. I remember picking up my bible and I just begin to read Matthew, Mark, Luke and John.

John1:1 In the beginning was the word, and the word was with God, and the word was God. I began to think about the word of God and how it has never changed. I thought about how God has always been the same, He did not change, I did.

I thought about my grandma and Val and got mad all over again. I began to contemplate on how things were way worst for my grandma but her faith never failed. She continued to trust and obey God despite her circumstances. She had loss her husband and had to bury not one, but two daughters. And here it is, I had not nearly been through what she had endured. I gave up on God at the first sight of trials. At this point. I should have dug my heels in deeper and held on to God's unchanging hand, but I let go. That is how we get sometimes when things do not go the way we think it should go, we give up, we through in the towel. When God only wants us to, " trust Him through the process, so that He can take us to the progress."

At this point, I was willing to try God. I had tried everything else and still felt empty, sad and alone. What did I have to lose? NOTHING from what I could see! I begin reading in Matthew 3:2 "And saying, repent ye: for the kingdom of heaven is at hand."I begin to read how Christ had came to this world to save the sinners. How He was the ultimate sacrifice.

My mind was slowly disappearing the more I read the word of God. It was not that this was the first time hearing it because I had heard it all before. I grew up in the church, so I knew the word of God. The Bible says in Proverbs 22:6 train up a child in the way he should go, and when he is old, he will not depart from it. See I was raised around the word and even though I allowed the world to take over my life by doing worldly things. The word of God was still deeply rooted in me from my mother, grandma and Big Ma instilling the word in me. I begin reading and wanting to have faith like both of my grandmothers. These were two women who believed and trusted God for everything.

I watch both praise Him even in the storms. They had raised 14 children a piece and never needed for anything because God always provided. I wanted that faith. I wanted to believe like they did. I went to see my Big Ma and she reassured me that God was all that I needed. She told me how she prayed daily, every morning, and night. She told me that the only way to her God was by reading his word. She told me that all I needed was the faith the size of a mustard seed. She told me with that little faith I could move a mountain. I remember she use to have me read the Bible to her when I would come visit her when I was little. I used to think she just wanted someone to read to her, but she really was having me to read the word of God so that I would have read the Bible for myself. Smart is what she was. All that time I thought I was helping her but really, I was helping myself by letting the word of God come out of my mouth. I was speaking the word of God. The word of God is always the same it will never come back void, you can bet your life on the word of God it will always remain the same.

Even then, me not knowing by simply reading the word out of my mouth, the devil had to flee. I was able to hear God's voice again; my trust began to come back by reading the word. My faith in God became stronger. The emptiness I use to feel began to be filled with the presence of the Holy Spirit. I no longer felt numb. I was able to feel the presence of God and I was willing to do everything to keep that feeling. I began going to church reading my Bible more. I stop hanging out and going to the club. I would go to a party every now and again but nothing where I was using drugs. At this point, my mind frame was, "I could serve God and still do some of the things I use to do." Not knowing that all Satan needs is a crack, and he will come in.

I began smoking weed again because I had allowed Satan to twist the word of God. I believed that it came from God and it was ok to smoke. I was reading my Bible and smoking weed, I was allowing the Devil to manipulate the situation. So many times, the devil will try to take the word of God and change it, but we must be smarter than that and know the word of God cannot be changed. I then stopped smoking and got my life back on track. No drugs, I was back seeking God with everything in me.

My life seemed to get better. Quincy proposed to me and we got married July 05, 2008. But that is when the enemy got mad and began to attack my body.

The Word of God helped me through.
THE HOLY BIBLE

PSALM 73:26; 26
My flesh and my heart may fail, but God is the strength of my heart and my portion forever.

1 CORINTHIANS 10:13-14 13
No temptation has overtaken you except what is common to mankind. And God is faithful; he will not let you be tempted
beyond what you can bear. But when you are tempted, he will also provide a
way out so that you can endure it. 14 Therefore, my dear friends, flee from
idolatry.

1 JOHN 2:16 16
For everything in the world—the lust of the flesh, the lust of the eyes, and the pride of life—comes not from the Father but from the world.

JAMES 4:7; 7
Submit yourselves, then, to God. Resist the devil, and he will flee from you.

1 CORINTHIANS 15:33; 33
Do not be misled: "Bad company corrupts good character."

1 CORINTHIANS 6:9-11; 9
Or do you not know that wrongdoers will not inherit the kingdom of God? Do not be deceived: Neither the sexually immoral nor idolaters nor adulterers nor men who have sex with men 10 nor thieves nor the greedy nor drunkards nor slanderers nor swindlers will inherit the kingdom of God. 11 And that is what some of you were. But you were washed, you were sanctified, you were justified in the name of the Lord Jesus Christ and by the Spirit of our God.

HEBREW 4: 15-16; 15
For we do not have a high priest who is unable to empathize with our weaknesses, but we have one who has been tempted in every way, just as we are—yet he did not sin. 16 Let us then approach God's throne of grace with confidence, so that we may receive mercy and find grace to help us in our time of need.

JOHN 3:15-16; 16
For God so loved the world that he gave his one and only Son, that whoever believes in him shall not perish but have eternal life. 17 For God did not send his Son

into the world to condemn the world, but to save the world through him.

PHILIPPIANS 4:13; 13
I can do all this through him who gives me strength.

Chapter 3

LUPUS: A DEATH SENTENCE

So here I am, happy planning my wedding, and pain would just come in my body and my body would freeze up, not allowing me to move. I kept going to the doctor all the while planning my wedding. July 05, 2008 came, and it was the happiest day of my life. Then approximately three days after I was married, I received the phone call that would change my life forever. The thought of that call still gives me chills today. I remember the doctor asking me was I sitting down she then went on to say she had run several tests and the results came back that I had Lupus with Rheumatoid arthritis. She went on to say that it was a terminal illness and that I would likely die from complication of this disease. I just sank down in the chair and began to cry. My first thought was why? Especially now that I had giving my life completely to God, I was married now, life as I knew it could not get no better. But that is how the enemy works just when you think everything is right, he comes in to kill steal and destroy. Satan wanted me to doubt God, to lose faith once again.

He wanted me to say why me again. But I was slowly learning WHY NOT me. I called Quincy and told him we needed to talk. We met at the house because when I got the call, I was at my mother's house. So, I went home and sat him down and begin to tell him what the doctor said. I went into details and told him that this was serious and that if he wanted out then he could because this was something he did not know about before the wedding. I told him that if he wanted to get our marriage annulled then we could I would understand. He went on to tell me that he loved me and that the vows he had said just three days before, he meant them and that he was going to stick with me through thick and thin, till death do us part. I knew I was going to have to find a doctor that specialized in Lupus to receive the best care.

So, I begin looking at Tuscaloosa, Alabama. I decided that we were moving to Alabama to be closer to my doctor. Plus, I had got a job at the hospital there working as a CNA. I was taking classes at the hospital to be a surgical tech. The hospital I worked at was a training hospital they would train you to do certain jobs then certify you. I was doing what I wanted to do and that was help people. Life was good despite Lupus it had not affected my body to bad, I was still able to do everything with no restrictions. I was going to work everyday loving my job. I got up one morning and had a bad headache. I remember taking something for it and going to work feeling dizzy. I continued going to work for about a week until the pain and dizziness got so bad, I could not function. Quincy took me to the ER where I was examined and told that I had viral meningitis. They came to this conclusion after they had performed a spinal tap. This is where they put a needle into your spine and draw out fluid from around your brain. I was in the hospital for two months.

The doctors had basically given upon me. The medicine they were giving me was not working. They could not figure out why I was still having the headaches and pain on such a great scale. At one point they had hooked wires up to my head trying o see what was happening inside my head still no answer. The doctors had given upon me. This was the first-time doctors told my husband that there was nothing else they could do but make me comfortable. I just knew I was going to die. I begin to pray. I was praying so hard. Quincy told me I was sleep but I was I remember praying out to God to come and save me. I could see a bright light at the foot of my hospital bed and a dark spirit on the left side of the bed. The dark spirit was saying he had me and that I was giving up and it was like God was saying no the battle is already won she just must believe, and I began to yell out of my mouth I choose you Lord. I begin asking God to save me. Now all while this is going on my husband and my cousin Demon who had came to see me was in the room watching me reach my hands out and saying I chose God.

They thought I was dreaming. But to me it was very much reality. I saw God telling Satan to take his hands off me that I was His. That I would live and not die. The voice of God began talking to me telling me that He had plans for me, that I would live and not die. Right there in my hospital bed I began to worship God. The nurses begin to come in the room I was praising God so loud. It was as if all the pain just left my body. My doctors were amazed at the turn around. They could not believe their eyes. I begin to gain my strength back. I had to go through physical therapy to walk again but I had God on my side, and nothing could defeat me. We moved back closer to home. I had gained my strength back I was doing good until one morning I got up to go to the bathroom. I used the bathroom and could not get up from the toilet. I tried several times to push myself up, but I could not. I yelled out to Quincy to come and help me. He came in the bathroom and said quit playing you just walked in here. I told him I am not playing. He proceeded to lift me up straight and when he let go, I fell to the ground. By this time, he begins to panic. He got me onto the bed and got me dressed and drove as fast as he could to the ER.

Upon arriving at the hospital, they took me to the back, and they ran several tests and saw that my potassium level was exceptionally low. Lupus had started to attack my kidneys they told us. They explained it to us that upon me going to the bathroom I was able to walk to the bathroom but when I used the bathroom my kidneys had flushed out the necessary potassium, I needed to make my muscles move. He begin to tell me that it looked like Lupus had started to affect my kidneys and I would need a kidney transplant if my kidneys continued to do this.

They admitted me in the hospital and began giving me potassium through an IV. It burned so bad. It was painful. That is when I learned that the body needed potassium to make my muscles work. My first thought was my heart, my heart is a muscle, fear began to take over my mind. Then I remember 2 Timothy 1:7 For God has not given us the spirit of fear, but of power and of love and of sound mind. I knew at that moment the enemy wanted me to feel fear not God. I had to tell myself that if God was allowing this to happen,

He was going to see me through it. I began to pray to God for strength to get through this. I prayed for healing, I asked God to heal my kidneys to allow them to function like they did when I was born. I stayed in the hospital for two weeks. They told me to follow up with a kidney doctor to begin the process of being put on the kidney list. My God had already begun to heal my body once again. I set the appointment with the doctor and went to my appointment the doctor looked at the test the hospital had ran and decided to run his own test to be sure he got the same diagnosis. I had to wait a week for the results to come back but when they did God had healed me. My doctor could not see what the hospital saw anymore. He told me I did not need to be put on the kidney list that my kidneys were functioning right, but lupus was causing my potassium to drop but it could be controlled with taking potassium daily. Once again God had moved in my favor. He had saved me, and I owed him my life. I got better and then we moved to Horn Lake MS. I had got a store management position and moved my family here.

My best friend at the time moved to the same apartments as me and it was great. My family and I had found a church home and things were going good again thanks to God.

The Word of God that helped me through this time:
THE HOLY BIBLE

ROMANS 5:3-5 3
Not only so, but we also glory in our sufferings, because we
know that suffering produces perseverance; 4 perseverance, character; and

character, hope. 5 And hope does not put us to shame, because God's love has
been poured out into our hearts through the Holy Spirit, who has been given
to us.

JAMES 1:2-3 2

Consider it pure joy, my brothers and sisters, whenever you
face trials of many kinds, 3 because you know that the testing of your faith
produces perseverance.

2 TIMOTHY 1:7

For God has not given us the spirit of fear, but of power and of love and of sound mind. I knew at that moment the enemy wanted me to feel fear not God.

JAMES 5:14-15; 14

"Is anyone among you sick? Let them call the elders of the church to pray over them and anoint them with oil in the name of the
Lord. And the prayer offered in faith will make the sick person well; the Lord will raise them up. If they have sinned, they will be forgiven."

JEREMIAH 30:17; 17

"But I will restore you to health and heal your wounds,' declares the LORD"

ISAIAH 54:10; 10

"So do not fear, for I am with you; do not be dismayed, for I am your God. I will strengthen you and help you; I will uphold you with my righteous right hand"

2 CHRONICLES 7:14-15; 14

"if my people, who are called by my name, will humble themselves and pray and seek my face and turn from their wicked ways, then I will hear from heaven, and I will forgive their sin and will heal their land. 15 Now my eyes will be open and my ears attentive to the prayers offered in this place."

ISAIAH 38: 16-17; 16

Lord, by such things people live; and my spirit finds life in the too. You restored me to health and let me live. 17 Surely it was for my benefit that I suffered such anguish. In your love you kept me from the pit of destruction; you have put all my sins behind your back."

Chapter 4

ENVY, JEALOUSY, WITHCRAFT & A Baby

Now before I jump into this chapter, let me tell you God had given me a vision several times in a dream of me having twin girls with my husband. My husband's request to God was to have a daughter by me because he felt like he already had three boys he was raising from my first marriage. So, in this dream I gave birth to two girls, one with a head full of hair and the other bald headed. Not sure why that stood out in my dream, but it did. My husband and I kept trying to conceive, no luck. We made an appointment with a doctor to check everything out. The doctor basically told us that because of lupus I would not be able to carry a child and he would not help us because of this. I was devastated again. Quincy begins to remind me of the vision God had given.

So, I went to my OBGYN and he ran several tests to see could I have a baby and he told us he did not see why we could not I did not have the antibody that would stop me from conceiving. I was relieved we began taking pills to help me conceive, we did artificial insemination everything no baby. I was exhausted. I begin to pray I told God I knew what he had showed me and when he was ready so would I. I got pregnant loss the baby at two months.

Got pregnant again back-to-back loss the baby three times. The last time I ended up getting pregnant in my tubes. I was rushed to surgery losing my right tube. Not even two months later New Year's Day January 1, 2013. I realized my cycle had not come on, so I took a at home pregnancy test. POSITIVE!! Ok now I am nervous I tell Quincy. He goes to the store buys two more test I take it, POSITIVE. So, I am still scared I tell Quincy lets go to the ER to make sure the baby is in the right place. We go and they confirm that I am 6 weeks pregnant and the baby is in the uterus I am so happy. In my mind, God had kept His promise this was going to be our twin girls. I began going to the doctor and because I had lupus, I had to have a high-risk doctor to monitor me and the baby. For five months of going to the doctor every week twice a week, once for me to be checked out then for the baby to be checked out. Every visit they would show me the baby moving, telling me it was a girl.

Everything was looking good they told me. Until one day I went to the doctor with whom at the time I thought was my best friend. That whole day was strange because she went to the doctor with me because she had told me she needed to talk to me about something. So, all the way to the doctor she never got into what she wanted to talk to me about. So, arriving at the doctor's office she told me she was going to stay in the car to smoke she was not coming in. Now that did not seem strange to me because she would do this all the time. I went into my appointment cheerful as usual the nurse began to do the ultrasound. Then she got quiet, and I asked her was everything ok? She responded that she was getting a lot of red flags with my baby. I asked her what red flags. She began to tell me that she saw a hole in the baby's heart, the baby's feet were cradle, and there was a hole in the spine of the baby's back.

She told me that she was going to put me in a room so the doctor could come and talk to me. The doctor came in and told me that it looked like my child had Trisomy 18 and it meant that if the baby lived, he/she would not live pass the age of 1. My heart just dropped in my lap. I asked him how we could be sure. He said that he would draw some of the amniotic fluid from my stomach, that would tell him everything about the baby from the sex to the genetic make-up.

He performed the test and told me it would take 7 to 10 days for the results to all be in and when all of them came in they would call me. I remember leaving the doctors office scared a little, but I had hoped that they were wrong once again. I did not say anything to my friend on the way home I just wanted to keep it between me and my husband until I found out the truth. She kept asking me what the doctor said I kept telling her everything was fine. I made it home prayed, waited on Quincy to come home to tell him the news. When he made it home, I told him everything the doctor said even the part about if the test results showed he had Trisomy 18, I would need to terminate the pregnancy because my body did not need to go through the strand of carrying a baby that was not going to live. Immediately

Quincy agreed with me that there was no way we would abort our baby. Even if the child only lived a day, that God would be the one to end his or her life not us.

Now during this wait time of uncertainty, I was in my Bible daily praying, reading the word of God. Whenever I am deep in the word of God, my discernment is extremely high, the Holy Spirit will not allow anything to get passed me. My so-called best friend came to tell me that her husband felt like my husband (Quincy) always looked at her. So, me being in my word like I was knew this was a lie. I went on to tell her that I knew that was a lie and that I did not care what her husband said that all I cared about was did she feel like he made her feel this way. She then she went on to tell me he had NEVER did anything to make her feel uncomfortable. She then began to tell me how much she loved me, and I told her I loved her too, she was my best friend and I saw her as a sister.

Now brace yourself for the demonic activity that is about to transpire!!

She told me no she loved me like a man loves a woman. I told her "Ain't no way in hell that was going to happen!" One, I was not attractive to women and two it was UNGODLY in every way. I told her that if she wanted a woman hey, I would help her find one but HELL to the Nawl!. That was not going to happen! I told her I had to go, and I ended that conversation. I saw then it was time to end this friendship. Over the next couple days, I stopped answering her phone calls. I did not need the extra stress, so I just stop answering calls from her.

THEN a few days later she showed up at my door with the phone in her hand telling me her sister wanted to speak with me. I took the phone, and her sister was on the phone telling me she missed our friendship and wanted us to start back talking and I explained to her that I did not have time for all the negativity that came alone with being her friend. By me reading my Bible, I was able to see her in a different light and that was just not the type of company I wanted to be around. Her sister said she understood because she was also pregnant and understood my focus should be on my health and the baby. By this time, she comes in takes the phone tells her sister bye and hang up. While I am looking at her, she has dirt all on her face. She asked me could she use my bathroom I told her yes. Now the way my apartment was made she made it to my boys' bathroom before she made it to mines. My bathroom was farther down the hallway. I did not miss the time she was gone.

And then, she came running up the hallway buck naked! She ran out of my apartment into the apartment parking lot with no clothes on. At this point, me and Quincy could not believe what had just happened. I ran to my bathroom to find a bloody tampon on the floor in front of the toilet, my shower water was running. I told Quincy to bring me my Bible and bleach. I began to pray over my bathroom I knew it was some type of witchcraft. I cleaned the bathroom and then I received a phone call from her husband saying she had taken her wedding ring off and left. I looked for it and could not find it at first, only to get in the shower that night after cleaning it with ammonia. When I looked up in my shower on the rim of the shower was her ring. I got out of the shower and took her the ring and her clothes that she had left. I knocked on her door she answers, and I told her that her plan would not work and to stay away from me in the name of Jesus.

The very next day, she moved out of the complex where I lived. Two days later I got the news that my child indeed had Trisomy 18 and it was a boy and that I needed to terminate the pregnancy. I fell in my hallway and just began to scream NO, LORD WHY? I was confused and angry with God I did not understand why He would allow something like this to happen. My boys called Quincy at work because I would not stop crying. He came home telling me to have faith God is going to bring us through this because we believed He would perform a miracle. I continued going to the doctor I would ask could the test be wrong; they would tell me no. The doctor told me one day that if the only thing that was wrong with my baby was the hole in his heart, he could go in and fix that, but it was too much wrong. I still believed that even if our son did not live nothing but a day it would be worth it, so I continued to carry him. I told God that when he was ready to take him, he would until then we were expecting a miracle.

August 6, 2013 was my birthday and me and two of my now best friends had taking me to eat Mexican for my birthday and I started having contraction at the table I was so excited. One of my friends worked at a doctor's office so she began to count my contraction they were getting faster and faster. They called Quincy he then took me to the hospital I was 36 weeks at the time so when I got there, they gave me a shot to stop the contraction. I went back home because they said I had four more weeks. On August 8, 2013, I was laying in the bed and I could feel three people climb into bed with me I started hollering Please do not take my baby repeatedly. Quincy ran in the room and told me I was sleeping I had to be dreaming. I began telling him no I was not sleep this was real I could feel something climbing into bed coming from different direction to kill my baby, he held me and told me I was dreaming. He managed to calm me down and I drifted off to sleep. I woke up that morning to him getting ready for work. Now every morning for nine months Hayden (the baby) would wake me up hungry craving frosted flakes. But this morning he did not. It startled me and I told Quincy that he was not moving, and it was strange because he would always do the same thing.

Quincy told me to drink some orange juice maybe he was sleep. So, he kissed me goodbye and went to work. It still bothers me, so I kept trying to get him to move by this time I noticed my feet and legs had swollen bad, so I called my doctor and the nurse told me to get to the ER immediately. My uncle Jason took me to the hospital where they took me to the back and the nurse came in and was talking to me saying she was going to do an ultrasound to check on the baby. She hooked me up to the monitor, but she could not find a heartbeat. I remember looking at the screen on the ultrasound machine and the image of my baby was balled up. The nurse ran out of the room and about four doctors ran in. They began to tell me to relax that they were trying to find the baby's heartbeat. One doctor asked me when the last time was, I felt the baby move and I told it was the night before. They kept trying to position the monitor to get a clear reading but was unable to. After trying for a while, the doctor said, I am sorry Mrs. Rupert but we cannot find a heartbeat the baby is no longer alive. I just began to scream, I was screaming and crying so loud that my uncle Jason came running down the hallway to find me in tears.

My heart was broken. They allowed me to call Quincy and my mom. I was just so hurt. I really did not have time to process what had happened was in a state of disbelief.

The doctors told me I would have to deliver the baby natural they did not want to put my body through the stress of performing a c-section. So, they induced my labor. It was the most painful labor I had ever had to experience. Because Hayden had died, I had to push him out by myself. I delivered him August 10, 2013 at 4:30a.m. When he came out it was as if I was having an outer body experience, I saw me in the bed the doctors and nurses around the bed. Quincy had backed into a corner crying and began to slide down the wall. My mother was in another corner crying. They were cleaning the baby off. Unbeknownst to me I had loss a lot of blood and was not doing good. I passed out to wake up to being given a huge amount of blood and platelets. But the doctors said I would be ok. They brought the baby to the room before the funeral home came to pick up the body. Here I was planning a funeral for our baby boy Hayden. He was supposed to be here with us. This was a different type of HURT. When the nurse placed him in my arms, Quincy was standing over me, we opened the blanket, crazy as it may seem, I wanted to see the things that they said were wrong with him. To my surprise everything that the told me was a lie. He did not have cradle feet or hands he did not have a hole in his stomach and back, his heart had just stopped. I cried; he did not have any of the facial features a Trisomy 18 baby would have. I told Quincy could it be that the doctors were seeing more than what was there. I pondered my mind with what my ex- friend had did. In my heart to this day, I feel like the doctors were made to see more through witchcraft than what was there.

If that was not enough, seven days passed, and we had not heard from the funeral home on the cremation of Hayden's remains. I called and they told me they were waiting on the hospital to clear the paperwork. I called the hospital and was told that was a lie, for them to pick up the body the paperwork was completed. By now, two weeks had passed and the funeral home is still giving me the run around. I called the hospital and got it in writing that everything on their end was complete. My concern was because bodies were coming up missing here at funeral homes, so I just knew they had lost Hayden's body. I had even told the funeral home I needed to see his body to make sure they had him. They told me," no" that his body had deteriorated and it would not be wise for me to see it. At this point, I felt they were lying because they were still saying they needed paperwork even after I showed them the paper from the hospital. I then contacted my local news and told them my story in a matter of two hours from when the story aired, I received a call from them saying my baby body was ready. I went to the funeral home with my boys to pick up the ashes. When I got there the owner apologized and told me a bunch of more lies. I got my son remains and got in the car. As I was driving away my son Jar'Quez asked me could he open the box I told him yes because I thought it was going to be just ashes to my surprise my son said mama, I see bones and rocks in here. I pulled over to the side of the road and just cried. When I looked at the bag, I could see bone fragments. When a cremation is done right there should not be anything but dust. I called my lawyer and filed a suit against the funeral home. My family and I went through months of counseling. At this point, I dove into my word deeper this time around I was going to trust God in every step I was not going to question him. I was learning to depend on him completely. I did not understand why but I had learned from the pass to trust God even the more when I could not see what was going to happen because he knew the ending. After months of deliberating, we won the case against the funeral home. We had loss so much over the last couple years, but I heard God saying I had to take you through some things to see if I could give you more. I had to endure some pain and hurt to get to where God could use me.

The Word of God that helped me through this time: THE HOLY BIBLE

2 Corinthians 1:3-12; 3

Praise be to the God and Father of our Lord Jesus Christ, the Father of compassion and the God of all comfort, 4 who comforts us in all our troubles, so that we can comfort those in any trouble with the comfort we ourselves receive from God. 5 For just as we share abundantly in the sufferings of Christ, so also our comfort abounds through Christ. 6 If we are distressed, it is for your comfort and salvation; if we are comforted, it is for your comfort, which produces in you patient endurance of the same sufferings we suffer. 7 And our hope for you is firm, because we know that just as you share in our sufferings, so also you share in our comfort. 8 We do not want you to be uninformed, brothers and sisters, about the troubles we experienced in the province of Asia. We were under great pressure, far beyond our ability to endure, so that we despaired of life itself. 9 Indeed, we felt we had received the sentence of death. But this happened that we might not rely on ourselves but on God, who raises the dead. 10 He has delivered us from such a deadly peril, and he will deliver us again. On him we have set our hope that he will continue to deliver us, 11 as you help us by your prayers. Then many will give thanks on our behalf for the gracious favor granted us in answer to the prayers of many. 12 Now this is our boast: Our conscience testifies that we have conducted ourselves in the world, and especially in our relations with you, with integrity and godly sincerity. We have done so, relying not on worldly wisdom but on God's grace.

JAMES 1:5-8

If any of you lacks wisdom, you should ask God, who gives generously to all without finding fault, and it will be given to you. 6 But when you ask, you must believe and not doubt, because the one who doubts is like a wave of the sea, blown and tossed by the wind. 7 That person should not expect to receive anything from the Lord. 8 Such a person is double-minded and unstable in all they do.

LUKE 1:37; 37

For no word from God will ever fail."

MARK 11:22-24; 22

"Have faith in God," Jesus answered. 23 "Truly I tell you, if anyone says to this mountain, 'Go, throw yourself into the sea,' and does not doubt in their heart but believes that what they say will happen, it will be done for them. 24 Therefore I tell you, whatever you ask for in prayer, believe that you have received it, and it will be yours.

1 CORINTHIANS 2:5; 5

so that your faith might not rest on human wisdom, but on God's power.

Philippians 4:13: 13
I can do all this through him who gives me strength.

PROVERBS 3:5-6; 5
Trust in the LORD with all your heart and lean not on your own understanding; 6 in all your ways submit to him, and he will make your paths straight.

Chapter 5

NEW HOUSE, NEW CAR, ACCEPTING MY CALLING & ADULTERY

It finally felt like the bad was behind me. We had gotten a new house built, and bought a new car. I was doing "Mornings with Kisha," praying on a prayer call three times a day with my WOG sisters, reading my word daily. Then one day, I was in my prayer room that I had built in my house and I was talking to God just like I am talking to you. And he asked me,
" When are you going to accept your calling?" I said God I have I am doing everything you asked me to do. He went on and said,
"Yes but you still are not accepting the calling as prophetess on your life."

I began to tell Him I do not have to have a title Lord I just want to serve you. God went on to say that He was not giving myself a title, but He was telling me who I was in His kingdom. I then told God, " Yes! YES, LORD"I said. " I WILL BE WHO YOU WANT ME TO BE." At that moment I could feel the presence of God all over me. It was a feeling I just cannot explain it was full of warmth and love. Then I heard God say,

"Now because you have accepted my calling, the devil is going to try you with your family." God told me that my husband was having an affair with a woman that was using witchcraft. He told me she had told my husband that she was pregnant but that was a lie. He told me that my son and I would have a great falling out and he would become very disobedient. He told me the people I trusted the most would betray me. I asked God, "What I can do?" The Lord told me that I had to keep my eyes on Him no matter what happened to continue to look to Him. I asked the Lord if my marriage was over? He told me no, and no matter what happen to continue to trust Him and He would see me through. Now after God had dropped all of this in my lap, He told me I could not say anything to my husband until he told me it was I noticed weeks passed and I began to see the signs of a cheating spouse.

One day while I was cooking, I heard God say, "Call him he is at her house now."

When I called, he did not answer but he called back? I asked him where he was and he asked "Why?" which was something we just did not do. I asked him where he was in the past, he would tell me. So, I told him to come home we needed to talk because God had giving me permission to say something now. When he came home, he had this arrogant spirit attached to him. An "I do not care attitude." I told him that I knew he was cheating, and I told him with who.

Now, he is looking at me with his eyes bucked wondering how I knew all this. I went on to tell him about the baby and that is when he was like Who told you this? I told him God. He just looked at me like I was crazy. I went on to tell him that she was not pregnant and that it was all a lie. See even then Satan was using my husband desires to trap him in this affair. Satan uses the things that we long after to tempt us into sin. I went on to tell my husband everything that God allowed me to say. I asked him did he love her. He told me he loves me. Over the next several days my life got flipped upside down. He began telling me he loves this woman, but he also loved me. I told him he could not continue to see this woman he had a choice to make. The next day I called his phone, and to my surprise she answered! We got into it and it was like everything holy in me left. I began to curse her and tell her I would kill her that I was not the one to play with. She started saying,

"Oh this cannot be the woman that prays three times a day on a prayer line."

The demon was taunting me, and I was falling right in her trap because I was ready to lay hands on him and her. Yes, me the woman of God who had just accepted my calling was saying she would kill someone.

By the time I made it home, he was pulling up. I asked him had he lost his mind allowing that women to answer his phone. When I looked at him, he did not even seem like the same person. He told me he loved her, and he loved me, and I just walked away from him. I wanted to hurt him like he had hurt me, but I could not. I went in the house and laid down only to be awaken out of my sleep to him trying to explain what happen and how he does not know what changed but he was in love with her. All of Kisha from the old days came up out of me.

"Ain't no way" I told him "you going to sit in my face and keep telling me you are in love with another women."

I took my eyes off God and began to deal with this in my flesh. I was so angry, I called this woman and told her to come get my husband. The woman kept asking me was I sure that I wanted her to come? I asked her, "Are you dumb? Come get him!"

At that moment, the shield of protection that God had over me and my family was lifted, I later found out. See that is why she kept asking was I sure. Because God had already told Satan he could not come to my dwelling but because I told her to come God had to take His hand off. I was not keeping my eyes on Him, I was letting what I heard and saw affect me. And my tunnel vision was getting cloudy because I was no longer acting off my faith in God but my flesh.

My husband left that night with her. The next day, I was on a prayer call praying and he walked back through the door to tell me that he loved me, and he could not understand why he said the things he had said. I knew it was witchcraft because God was still telling what was going on. We prayed over him me and my WOG sisters he was laying in the bed in a fetal position like he was in a daze his phone began to ring. I answered it and it was her wanting to speak to him. I began speaking out of my mouth that every spell she had use was null and void and to no attempt in the mighty name of Jesus. She called back-to-back that day asking to speak to him and begging me to have him to call her mother. I knew then the mother had to be the one casting the spell. I started praying against her as well. During my storm, God was allowing her to tell on herself so I would know what to pray for. I began commanding that every witch die because in Exodus 22:18 thou shalt not a witch to live. A day later, I woke up to find a broken bottle at my doorstep that had something yellow and red in it, that day my husband left and parked my car in the middle of the road in our neighborhood. My heart once again was broken. I went to God and asked why He did not tell me my husband was going to leave me, and what God said to me changed my mind frame about everything. See in the beginning, God told me to keep my eyes on him. That no matter what it seemed like to keep my eyes on him. He told me not to look at the things that were happening and I did. I let flesh make me step out of character. By me stepping out of character I was stepping out of the grace of God. But let me tell you how good my God is, even though God said you did this. I am still going to save your husband. He said and when I bring him back, he will be better. I SURRENDERED that day to God. God showed me that what ever was in that glass that was broken on my doorstep that this woman left was a spell to make my husband not come back.

After I surrendered it all to God that day, three months had passed. Quincy was calling and texting. Everyday I was telling him to come home we could work it out. Everybody was telling me to act up, do what he was doing but I could not God had a hold on me. And I was not about to mess up again acting out.

There were days I cried all day. And then suddenly, the tears stopped, and I dedicated all my energy to God, I was no longer waiting on my husband to come home. All I knew was I had found a new love and it was CHRIST JESUS. The first three months, he was gone I was crying everyday sick, could not walk because my Lupus was flaring up, angry at myself because I was dependent on him, I was not working. He had closed all the bank accounts. I did not know how I was going to pay my bills. But God stepped in and fixed everything I started making money selling plates and doing credit repair. God had made a way for me to pay my bills and take care of my kids.

The next three months I was so focused on pleasing GOD; I was not worried about my marriage. I stopped answering every call from him. I stop responding to text messages. My focus was God. God even had me telling what I was going through with my husband on Facebook. Not realizing that other women all over the world were going through what I was going through. Women from New York, Chicago, Africa would inbox me on messenger to tell me that my testimony was helping them. I told my husband that I refused to be alone for the holidays if he had not come back home and ended this then I was filing for my divorce and moving on with my life. On Thanksgiving morning my husband came home. It took God for me to put a side all the things that happen. God had told me over the course of that storm that He was going to bring my husband back and I believed that, and He did just that. My husband has been back home now for three years. Everyday God shows me how he is changing him. He is now on the prayer call with me. He even has his own night to where he conducts Prayer call. The change in him is not by anything I have done but by everything God did. He prays with me and for me. He also prays over me when I am not feeling well. I honestly believe that there is no task to big for God or impossible.

Today I speak healing over my body because I genuinely believe in my heart that God has healed me, I am just waiting on manifestation.

The Word of God that helped me through this time:
THE HOLY BIBLE

PHILIPPIANS 4:13; 13
I can do all this through him who gives me strength.

MATTHEW 21:22; 22
If you believe, you will receive whatever you ask for in prayer."

1 CORINTHIANS 6:9
Know ye not that the unrighteous shall not inherit the kingdom of God? Be not deceived: neither fornicators, nor idolaters, nor adulterers, nor effeminate, nor abusers of themselves with mankind,

Deuteronomy 22:22 -
If a man be found lying with a woman married to an husband, then they shall both of them die, [both] the man that lay with the woman, and the woman: so shalt thou put away evil from Israel.

LEVITICUS 20:10 -
And the man that committeth adultery with [another] man's wife, [even he] that committeth adultery with his neighbour's wife, the adulterer and the adulteress shall surely be put to death.

PSALMS 6:32 -
[But] whoso committeth adultery with a woman lacketh
understanding: he [that] doeth it destroyeth his own
soul.

LUKE 16:18 -
Whosoever putteth away his wife, and marrieth
another,
committeth adultery: and whosoever marrieth her
that is put away from [her] husband committeth adultery.

MATTHEW 19:9 -
And I say unto you, Whosoever shall put away his
wife, except [it be] for fornication, and shall marry
another, committeth adultery: and whoso marrieth her
which is put away doth commit adultery.

Matthew 5:28 -
But I say unto you, That whosoever looketh on a
woman to lust after her hath committed adultery with
her already in his heart.

LUKE 17: 3-4; 3
Take heed to yourselves: If thy brother trespass
against thee, rebuke him; and if he repent, forgive him. 4
And if he trespass against thee seven times in a day, and
seven times in a day turn again to thee, saying, I repent;
thou shalt forgive him.

ISAIAH 1:18 -

Come now, and let us reason together, saith the LORD: though your sins be as scarlet, they shall be as white as snow; though they be red like crimson, they shall be as wool.

LEVITICUS 19:31; 31
" 'Do not turn to mediums or seek out spiritists, for you will be defiled by them.
I am the LORD your God.

LEVITICUS 20:6; 6
" 'I will set my face against anyone who turns to mediums and spiritists to prostitute themselves by following them, and I will cut them off from their people.

LEVITICUS 20:27; 27
" 'A man or woman who is a medium or spiritist among you must be put to death. You are to stone them; their blood will be on their own heads.'

MICAH 5:10-12; 10
"In that day," declares the LORD, "I will destroy your horses from among you and demolish your chariots. 11 I will destroy the cities of your land and tear down all your strongholds. 12 I will destroy your witchcraft and you will no longer cast spells.

CONCLUSION

I wrote this book because God told me the things that I had been through were not about me but about the people I would turn to Him. There were times throughout my 40 years on this earth I wanted to know why I had endured so much pain. In certain situations, I had not done anything to deserve some of the things that was upon me. God had to remind me of his son Jesus. See Jesus had not done anything to anyone to receive the treatment he received. He was without fault or sin so who was I? If my lord and savior had encountered hardship, scandalize his name, lied on and so much more who was I that I could not be did the same. For he was the SON OF GOD, THE PRINCE OF PEACE, MY SAVIOR. I realized it was not about me at all.

For the work of the kingdom had to be done, I had a calling on my life, I had to go through something and I had to be tested to see if I was worthy to carry the mantle God had placed over my life. Me not knowing any time that I had to be in sackcloth and ashes to receive the anointing that God had for me. Everything I went through was painful, hurtful. I would not wish it on no one, was worth it. If I had to do it all over again I would because of who I am now. Which is SAVED, SANCTIFIED AND DELIVERED. I AM FREE TRULY FREE INDEED.

I tell people who ask me how I made it, "This walk isn't for the squeamish" as my war sister Carolyn would say. But its worth it and it can be done with God by your side. I used to be so hurt about the things I was going through but God sent me a woman of God by the name Carolyn Orr who would pray for me, pray with me and tell me how God helped her through. Believe me when I say whatever you ask God for, He will supply. I needed someone that would do those things as well as tell me the truth even when I was wrong or right. But always Godly wisdom. When I went through what I went through with my husband, She told me to listen to God and to do whatever he told me. See God told me he was going to bring my husband back better that ever but I had family and friends telling me to move on, but instead I trusted God and He did just what He said He was going to do. I am grateful that I waited on God's promise to me.

So, trust Him in everything that you do. In times of good and trouble lean on God. Trust Him even when you cannot see what He is telling you. For He knows the beginning and the end.

www.ingramcontent.com/pod-product-compliance
Lightning Source LLC
Chambersburg PA
CBHW062141280426
43673CB00072B/92